# NORTHWEST
# Mountain Wildflowers

**Dana Visalli ◆ Walt Lockwood ◆ Derrick Ditchburn**

hancock

house

ISBN 0-88839-516-7
Copyright © 2005 Hancock House Publishers

**Cataloging in Publication Data**
Visalli, Dana, 1948–
　Northwest mountain wildflowers / Dana Visalli, Walt Lockwood, Derrick Ditchburn.

(Northwest wildflower series)
Includes index.
ISBN 0-88839-516-7

　1. Wild flowers—Northwest, Pacific—Identification. 2. Mountain plants—Northwest, Pacific—Identification. I. Lockwood, Walt, 1938– II. Ditchburn, Derrick, 1934– III. Title. IV. Series.

QK144.V584 2005　　　582'.13'0979509143　　　C2004-901829-9

Printed in South Korea—PACOM

Editor: Dana Visalli
Photography: Dana Visalli, Walt Lockwood, Derrick Ditchburn,
　　　　David Hancock, Don McPhee & Mildred McPhee
Production: Rick Groenheyde, Laura Michaels, Theodora Kobald

Published simultaneously in Canada and the United States by

**HANCOCK HOUSE PUBLISHERS LTD.**
19313 Zero Avenue, Surrey, B.C. Canada V3S 9R9
(604) 538-1114　Fax (604) 538-2262

**HANCOCK HOUSE PUBLISHERS**
1431 Harrison Avenue, Blaine, WA U.S.A 98230-5005
(604) 538-1114　Fax (604) 538-2262

*Website:* www.hancockhouse.com
*Email:* sales@hancockhouse.com

# Contents

# INTRODUCTION

*L*ate April and May are exciting times in the mountains of the Pacific Northwest. Winter's blanket of snow is in retreat, and the early spring wildflowers are emerging in midelevation meadows. By late June we can venture higher into the subalpine zone to enjoy another round of spring blooms. In July and August, when coastal and inland flowers are withering under the summer sun, alpine wildflowers are reaching a crescendo of color, as ridges, scree slopes, meadows and mountain peaks play host to a wealth of floral beauties.

The purpose of this introductory guidebook is to assist in identifying and enjoying mountain wildflowers from southern Alaska to northern Oregon. This is a vast area for a small book, so we have focused on the most common mountain species within our range.

The book is simple to use, as flowers are arranged by color. For most species there are two images, including a closeup of the flower and a view of the entire plant.

Text is kept to a minimum, as are technical botanical terms. **Annuals** die every year, leaving only seeds, whereas **perennials** die back to the ground but persist underground. **Sepals** are the bracts around the outside of the petals; they cover the flower bud before it opens. Usually sepals are green; occasionally they are the same color as the petals. **Corolla** refers to all the petals of a flower, taken together. **Compound leaves** refers to leaves that are divided into a number of separate leaflets. If the leaflets are all joined together at a common point, like the fingers on a hand, they are **palmately compound**. If they are joined in twos opposite one another, they are **pinnately compound**. The scientific name for each plant is given, because common names vary from place to place. Even some scientific names change over time.

John Muir once remarked that all he needed for an adventure was to put "some bread and tea in an old sack and jump over the back fence." All you need for a fine adventure is this little book and a mountain meadow.

# WESTERN ANEMONE, WESTERN PASQUEFLOWER

*Anemone occidentalis*

**Plant:** A tufted perennial 10-60 cm tall, blooming soon after snow melt, has a distinctive, fuzzy seedhead.

**Flower:** No petals, but white to purplish sepals are petal-like, 2-3 cm long, flower has numerous stamens and pistils.

**Fruit:** Numerous achenes with long feathery styles, creating showy, beard-like heads.

**Leaves:** Mostly basal, long-stalked, deeply divided into pointed segments.

**Habitat:** Widespread in alpine and subalpine meadows, and on rocky slopes.

**Range:** B.C. to California.

# MISTMAIDEN

*Romanzoffia sitchensis*

**Plant:** A delicate, tufted perennial 5-30 cm tall, often mistaken for a saxifrage, it is in the waterleaf family.

**Flower:** White and bell-shaped, with a yellow center or 'eye', few to several blossoms at the end of weak, thin stems.

**Leaves:** Mostly basal with roundish, coarsely toothed blades 1-4 cm wide.

**Habitat:** On wet, gravelly slopes and ledges in alpine and subalpine zones.

**Range:** Alaska to California.

5

# SPOTTED SAXIFRAGE

*Saxifraga bronchialis*

**Plant:** Dense, matted cushions with erect flowering stems to 15 cm.

**Flower:** 5 petals 5-7 mm long with purple and orange spots, numerous flowers on erect stems.

**Leaves:** Basal and alternate, leathery, lance-shaped to oblong, with fine hairs along the margins.

**Habitat:** Common on rocky ridges and slopes, rock crevices, mainly alpine, sometimes midelevation.

**Range:** Alaska to Oregon.

# LEATHERLEAF SAXIFRAGE

*Leptarrhena pyrolifolia*

**Plant:** An erect, mat-forming perennial with unbranched, red, glandular-hairy stems 20-40 cm tall.

**Flower:** Small white flowers are in dense clusters at tip of stems, the 5 petals 2-3 mm.

**Fruit:** Two bright, purplish-red capsules.

**Leaves:** Basal, oval to elliptical, leathery, shiny, and serrate.

**Habitat:** In wet areas, seepages, streamsides, from mid- to subalpine zones.

**Range:** Alaska to Oregon.

# ALPINE SAXIFRAGE

*Saxifraga tolmei*

**Plant:** A low, mat-forming succulent with numerous, erect flowering stems 3-8 cm tall.
**Flower:** White, normally solitary on the stem, with 5 well-separated petals, 5 white stamens (filaments are white, anthers are reddish).
**Leaves:** 3-10 mm long, rounded to spoon shaped, fleshy, forming a succulent mat.
**Habitat:** Rocky slopes, ridges, cliffs, from sea level to alpine tundra.
**Range:** Alaska to California.

# WESTERN SAXIFRAGE

*Saxifraga occidentalis*

**Plant:** Perennial with solitary, leafless stems 15-35 cm tall, arising from basal rosettes.
**Flower:** Petals 1.5-3.5 mm, white to pink with 2 yellow spots at base, numerous flowers in an open or crowded, upright inflorescence.
**Leaves:** All basal, elliptical to egg-shaped, coarsely toothed, 3-8 cm long.
**Habitat:** Inhabits moist subalpine and alpine meadows, and rocky ridges.
**Range:** B.C. to Oregon.

7

# RUSTY SAXIFRAGE

*Saxifraga ferruginea*

**Plant:** An upright, branching perennial 10-40 cm tall.

**Flower:** White to purple with 5 asymmetrically arranged petals 4-6 mm long, the upper 3 larger than the lower and with 2 yellow spots apiece.

**Leaves:** All basal, club-shaped and deeply but irregularly toothed, 2-10 cm long.

**Habitat:** Primarily in rocky, often moist sites, from lowlands to alpine.

**Range:** Alaska to California.

# HEART-LEAVED SAXIFRAGE

*Saxifraga punctata*

**Plant:** A mat-forming perennial of wet ground, with hairy but non-glandular stems 15-40 cm tall.

**Flower:** 5 symmetrically arranged white petals narrowed at the base, 2.5-3.5 mm long, flowers with thickened, white filaments and red-purple styles.

**Leaves:** All basal, circular to kidney-shaped, indented at the stem, coarsely toothed around the margin, on long stalks.

**Habitat:** Rocky slopes, seepages, and stream-banks from mid- to alpine elevations.

**Range:** Alaska to Oregon.

# STREAM SAXIFRAGE

*Saxifraga arguta*

**Plant:** A matted perennial of wet ground, with glandular stems growing from 20-50 cm tall.

**Flower:** 5 asymmetrically arranged white petals narrowed at the base, 3-4 mm long, flowers with thickened white filaments and red-purple styles.

**Leaves:** All basal, kidney-shaped, coarsely toothed around the margin, on long stalks.

**Habitat:** Stream banks, seepages and among moist rocks at mid- to high elevations.

**Range:** Alaska to California.

# LYALL'S SAXIFRAGE

*Saxifraga lyallii*

**Plant:** A matted perennial with leafless, red-purple stems 15-25 cm tall.

**Flower:** A few small, white, asymmetrical flowers clustered at the end of red stems, the filaments white and flattened, petals 2.5-4 mm.

**Leaves:** Spoon-shaped and coarsely toothed, on long stems, the blades 1-2.5 cm long.

**Habitat:** Stream banks, seepages, and other moist areas in alpine and subalpine zones.

**Range:** Alaska to Washington.

## CASCADE MOUNTAIN-ASH

*Sorbus scopulina*

**Plant:** An erect, branching shrub 2-5 m tall.

**Flower:** Many very small, white flowers, bunched together in flat-topped clusters to 8 cm across.

**Fruit:** Small, round, clustered, red-orange fruits, edible but bitter.

**Leaves:** Pinnately compound leaves with 9-15 yellow-green, sharp-pointed leaflets.

**Habitat:** Open forests, avalanche tracks, occasionally in subalpine meadows.

**Range:** Alaska to California.

**Note:** The similar Sitka mountain ash (*Sorbus sitchensis*) has 7-11 rounded leaflets.

## WESTERN TEA-BERRY

*Gaultheria ovatifolia*

**Plant:** A low, creeping evergreen shrub with trailing branches that root at the nodes, to 5 cm tall.

**Flower:** Small (3.5-5 mm long) and bell shaped, white to pale pink, borne on the under side of branches in leaf axils.

**Fruit:** The bright red berries are edible.

**Leaves:** The ovate, leathery, toothed leaves are evergreen and alternate on the stem, 1.5-4 cm long.

**Habitat:** Moist forest, meadows and wetlands at middle to subalpine elevations.

**Range:** B.C. to California.

# SITKA VALERIAN

*Valeriana sitchensis*

**Plant:** An upright perennial with squared, rather succulent stems 20-100 cm tall.

**Flower:** Many small white to pink flowers gathered in a rounded or flat-topped cluster at the end of long, upright stems.

**Leaves:** Compound leaves opposite one another on the stem, the larger ones with 5 leaflets, the terminal leaflet the largest.

**Habitat:** Moist meadows, open forests and streambanks, mid- to high elevations.

**Range:** Alaska to California.

# MOUNTAIN BISTORT

*Polygonum bistortoides*

**Plant:** Perennial with 1 to several erect flowering stems 10-70 cm tall.

**Flower:** Very small, white to pink flowers gathered together in a tight, cylindrical cluster at the top of an almost leafless stem.

**Leaves:** Most leaves are long-stalked and basal, with oblong blades 5-15 cm long, the stem leaves are few, smaller, and sessile (stalkless).

**Habitat:** In moist subalpine to alpine meadows.

**Range:** B.C. to California.

# ALPINE BUCKWHEAT

*Eriogonum pyrolifolium*

**Plant:** A tufted sub-shrub (with a woody base) 4-15 cm tall.

**Flower:** Many small (4-6 mm) flowers gathered into rounded clusters 3-8 cm across, the stems leafless except for 2 linear bracts below the inflorescence.

**Leaves:** Basal, elliptic, 1.5-4 cm long, grayish-hairy below.

**Habitat:** Dry scree and rocky ridges at high elevations.

**Range:** Washington to California.

**Note:** The unusual odor of the flowers gives rise to the common name 'dirty sox.'

## ERICACEAE · HEATHER FAMILY
# WHITE-VEINED WINTERGREEN
*Pyrola picta*

**Plant:** An evergreen perennial with red-brown flowering stems 10-30 cm tall.

**Flower:** Several cream to yellow flowers atop a naked stem, each with 5 petals 5-10 mm long and a red, down-curved style.

**Leaves:** Several elliptical, basal leaves 2-7 cm long, usually notably bi-colored, with green blades and whitish veins.

**Habitat:** Dry to moist forests at low to subalpine elevations.

**Range:** B.C. to California.

## POLYGONACEAE · BUCKWHEAT FAMILY
# SULFUR FLOWER, SULFUR BUCKWHEAT
*Eriogonum umbellatum*

**Plant:** A mat-forming perennial 5-40 cm tall.

**Flower:** Tiny 2 mm white or yellow flowers in crowded, globose heads, the stem leafless except for a whorl of leaf-like bracts below the flowers.

**Leaves:** Ovate-elliptic, 1-3 cm long, in whorls at base of stem, often shiny-green above and gray-hairy below.

**Habitat:** Dry, open places from sage-steppe to alpine ridges.

**Range:** B.C. to California.

13

## PARRY'S CATCHFLY

*Silene parryi*

**Plant:** Perennial with several clustered stems 15-30 cm high, sticky, gland-tipped hairs cover the plant.

**Flower:** 5 white petals, each one with 4 lobes, the flowers borne in groups of 3-7 at stem tip and in leaf axils, the sepals are green to purplish and fused together into a tube.

**Leaves:** Basal and opposite one another on the stem, narrowly elliptical to linear, 3-8 cm long.

**Habitat:** Dry, rocky ridges and open meadows, montane to subalpine zone.

**Range:** B.C. to Washington.

## SPRINGBEAUTY

*Claytonia lanceolata*

**Plant:** A delicate, fleshy perennial 5-20 cm tall.

**Flower:** 5 white to pink, spreading petals are often pink-lined, 6-12 mm long, with only 2 sepals, several flowers per stem.

**Leaves:** Several lance-shaped basal leaves and 2 opposite lanceolate or elliptical leaves near middle of stem.

**Habitat:** Sage-steppe to alpine meadows.

**Range:** B.C. to California.

# NARROW-LEAVED COTTON-GRASS

*Eriophorum polystachion*

**Plant:** Upright, grass-like, rhizomatous, perennial plants 15-70 cm tall.

**Flower:** 2 to several drooping, cottony heads composed of clusters of minute florets.

**Fruit:** Brown to black seeds are surrounded by many long, silky-white, cottony bristles.

**Leaves:** Narrow, grass-like leaves 5-20 cm long, both at base and along stem.

**Habitat:** Bogs and wet meadows from lowlands to subalpine.

**Range:** Alaska to Oregon.

# PARTRIDGEFOOT

*Luetkea pectinata*

**Plant:** A low-growing, mat-forming perennial to 15 cm tall.

**Flower:** Many small, white flowers with protruding stamens clustered together at the top of a leafy stem.

**Leaves:** Small, primarily basal leaves are 2-3 times divided into fine segments, ostensibly resembling the toes of a partridge.

**Habitat:** Meadows and rocky slopes in subalpine and alpine zones.

**Range:** Alaska to California.

## ALPINE MARSHMARIGOLD

*Caltha leptosepala*

**Plant:** A fleshy-leaved, glabrous (hairless) perennial of wet ground, 5-35 cm tall.

**Flower:** Petals absent, but the 6-12 white sepals appear as petals, the flower center yellow, typically 1 flower per stem.

**Leaves** Mostly basal, round to heart-shaped, longer than wide, coarsely toothed, 5-10 cm long.

**Habitat:** Along streams and in seepage areas from montane forest into alpine zones, frequently forms dense populations, blooms early in the season.

**Range:** B.C. to Oregon.

**Note:** Similar to white marsh-marigold and something of a challenge to tell the two apart.

## THREAD-LEAVED SANDWORT

*Arenaria capillaris*

**Plant:** A mat-forming perennial 10-25 cm tall, the mats 5-20 cm wide.

**Flower:** 5 white, rounded, white petals 6-10 mm long and 5 pink stamens, 1-10 flowers per stalk, sepals purple-tinged, stems glandular.

**Leaves:** Many linear basal leaves 2-4 cm long, stem leaves in pairs, opposite one another.

**Habitat:** In open areas from sagebrush plains to sub-alpine slopes.

**Range:** B.C. to Oregon.

# WHITE MARSHMARIGOLD

*Caltha biflora*

**Plant:** A fleshy-leaved, glabrous (hairless) perennial of wet ground, 5-35 cm tall.

**Flower:** Petals absent, but the 6-12 white sepals appear as petals, the flower center yellow, typically 2-3 flowers per stem.

**Leaves:** Mostly basal, circular to kidney-shaped, as wide or wider than long, coarsely toothed, 5-10 cm long.

**Habitat:** Along streams and in seepage areas from montane forest into alpine zones, frequently forms dense populations, blooms early in the season.

**Range:** B.C. to Oregon.

CRUCIFERAE · MUSTARD FAMILY

# ALPINE SMELOWSKIA

*Smelowskia calycina*

**Plant:** A low-growing, densely matted, gray-hairy perennial, 5-20 cm tall.

**Flower:** 4 white to pink petals 4-8 mm long, flowers clustered in heads top a leafy stem.

**Leaves:** A basal mat and alternate on flower stem, pinnately compound, blue-gray and hairy, 1-10 cm long.

**Habitat:** Ridges, rock crevices and talus slopes in the alpine zone.

**Range:** B.C. to Washington.

**17**

## ALPINE WINTERGREEN
*Gaultheria humifusa*

**Plant:** Dwarf evergreen shrub, stems up to 10 cm long.

**Flower:** Small (3-5 mm) white to pink, urn-shaped flowers are solitary in the leaf axils.

**Leaves:** Broadly ovate, 1-2 cm long, alternate along the stem.

**Habitat:** Forests and moist slopes in the alpine and subalpine zones.

**Range:** B.C. to Oregon.

**Note:** The very similar western teaberry, (*Gaultheria ovatifolia*, page 10), has a hairy calyx (the fused sepals), while the calyx of alpine wintergreen is glabrous.

## GLOBEFLOWER
*Trollius laxus*

**Plant:** An upright perennial of wet ground, 10-50 cm tall.

**Flower:** Petals absent, but the 5-12 white sepals are petal-like, 12-16 mm long with numerous stamens coloring the center yellow, flowers are solitary at stem tips.

**Leaves:** The several basal leaves are on long stems and palmately divided into 5 toothed segments, there is one or more smaller leaves just below the flower.

**Habitat:** Wet meadows and streambanks in the subalpine and alpine zones.

**Range:** B.C. to Washington.

# MOUNTAIN MARIPOSA LILY

*Calochortus subalpinus*

**Plant:** A narrowly upright perennial 10-30 cm tall.

**Flower:** 3 obovate, white to yellowish petals 2-3 cm long, the 3 underlying sepals usually each with a purple dot at the base.

**Leaves:** A single, narrow, grass-like leaf halfway up the stem.

**Habitat:** Open forests and meadows at mid- to subalpine elevations.

**Range:** Washington to Oregon.

**Note:** Very similar to Tolmie's mariposa lily, *Calochortus tolmiei*.

# DWARF BRAMBLE

*Rubus lasiococcus*

**Plant:** A dwarf perennial 3-10 cm high, the trailing stems up to 2 m long, rooting at the nodes, plant lacks prickles.

**Flower:** 5 white petals 7-15 mm long, flowers are often in pairs.

**Fruit:** Small, edible berries are red and hairy.

**Leaves:** 3-lobed, rounded and toothed, 3-6 cm wide.

**Habitat:** Understory species in mid- to high elevation forests.

**Range:** B.C. to California.

**19**

## PINEDROPS
*Pterospora andromedea*

**Plant:** A narrowly upright, sticky-hairy perennial to 1 m tall, this reddish-brown saprophyte obtains its carbohydrates from dead organic material in the soil rather than from photosynthesis.

**Flower:** Numerous small (5-8 mm) yellow to red, urn-shaped flowers hang down from an elongate stalk.

**Leaves:** Small and scale-like, on the lower stem.

**Habitat:** Humus-rich soil in low to midelevation coniferous forests.

**Range:** Alaska to California.

## BIRCH-LEAVED SPIRAEA
*Spiraea betulifolia*

**Plant:** An upright, narrowly-branching shrub 20-100 cm tall.

**Flower:** Numerous small (3 mm long) rose flowers with protruding pink stamens grow together in dense, round or flat-topped clusters.

**Leaves:** Oval to oblong leaves are 3-6 cm long, coarsely serrate at the tip, tapering to the stalk, alternate up the stem.

**Habitat:** Open forests to open hillsides, from low forest to sub-alpine elevations.

**Range:** B.C. to Oregon.

# FENDLER'S WATERLEAF

*Hydrophyllum fendleri*

**Plant:** A perennial 20-80 cm tall, typically forming a thick mass of leaves.

**Flower:** Clusters of small (6-10 mm) white flowers with hairy sepals and protruding stamens stand upright or droop among leaves.

**Leaves:** Sharply toothed leaves 10-25 cm long divided into 7-15 pointed leaflets.

**Habitat:** Meadows and thickets mid- to subalpine elevations.

**Range:** B.C. to California.

# MOUNTAIN LADY'S-SLIPPER

*Cypripedium montanum*

**Plant:** An upright, branching perennial 20-70 cm tall.

**Flower:** White, bulbous lower petal forms a pouch, framed by long, narrow, copper-colored sepals.

**Leaves:** Elliptic and parallel-veined, 6-15 cm long, alternating up the flower stem.

**Habitat:** Dry to moist open forests, low to midelevations, typically where soil is moist in spring.

**Range:** Alaska to California.

21

# ROUND-LEAVED ALUMROOT
*Heuchera cylindrica*

**Plant:** A tufted perennial 10-40 cm tall.

**Flower:** Colored by the 5 cream to yellow sepals, 6-10 mm long, the petals smaller, sometimes lacking, flowers clustered in tight heads at the end of leafless stalk.

**Leaves:** In a basal rosette on long stalks, rounded, lobed and toothed, 1-8 cm long.

**Habitat:** Rocky soil, cliffs and talus slopes, low to midelevations.

**Range:** B.C. to California.

ROSACEAE · ROSE FAMILY

# WILD STRAWBERRY
*Fragaria virginiana*

**Plant:** A low, spreading perennial 4-10 cm high.

**Flower:** 5 white petals 5-10 mm long frame a yellow center.

**Fruit:** A small edible strawberry.

**Leaves:** Compound with 3 toothed leaflets, with the terminal tooth usually shorter than side ones, the leaf blade not bulging upward between veins.

**Habitat:** Open forests and meadows, low to midelevations.

**Range:** Alaska to California.

## ROSACEAE · ROSE FAMILY

# WOODLAND STRAWBERRY

*Fragaria vesca*

**Plant:** A low, spreading perennial 4-10 cm high.

**Flower:** 5 white petals 5-10 mm long frame, a yellow center.

**Fruit:** A small, edible strawberry.

**Leaves:** Compound with 3 toothed leaflets, with the terminal tooth usually longer than side ones, the leaf blade bulging upward between veins.

**Habitat:** Open forests and meadows, low to subalpine elevations.

**Range:** B.C. to California.

## LILIACEAE · LILY FAMILY

# SCALLOPED ONION

*Allium crenulatum*

**Plant:** A low-growing perennial to 10 cm tall.

**Flower:** The 6 white to pink tepals are 6-12 mm long and have a pink midvein, the flowers clustered on stalk above leaves.

**Leaves:** Typically 2 long, flattened leaves curving outward from stem.

**Habitat:** Rocky ridges, outcrops and gravel areas, normally alpine, though occasionally in lowlands.

**Range:** B.C. to Oregon.

**23**

## HEART-LEAVED TWAYBLADE
*Listera cordata*

**Plant:** A small, slender perennial with a solitary stem 6-20 cm tall.

**Flower:** 6-16 green to purple flowers distributed along upper stem, the lower petal of each split into 2 lance-shaped teeth.

**Leaves:** A single pair of heart-shaped leaves opposite one another on stem.

**Habitat:** Coniferous forests, along streams and in bogs, low to high elevations.

**Range:** Alaska to California.

## STAR-FLOWERED SOLOMON'S SEAL
*Smilacina stellata*

**Plant:** An upright to leaning perennial 20-60 cm tall, sometimes forming spreading colonies.

**Flower:** 5-20 small (1-1.5 cm wide), white, star-like flowers with 6 narrow tepals at end of stem.

**Fruits:** Green fruit turns bright red when ripe.

**Leaves:** Lanceolate, alternate on flower stalk, 5-16 cm long and 1-5 cm wide.

**Habitat:** Moist woods and streams to dry, open hillsides.

**Range:** Alaska to California.

24

# SILVERLEAF PHACELIA
*Phacelia hastata*

**Plant:** A upright to sprawling silver-green perennial 10-50 cm tall.

**Flower:** Numerous small (4-8 mm) white to purple flowers are tightly clustered, with anthers protruding conspicuously.

**Leaves:** Gray-hairy and elliptic, with prominent veins, 5-12 cm long, basal and along stem.

**Habitat:** Sage-steppe to Douglas-fir forest.

**Range:** B.C. to California.

# NUTTALL'S SANDWORT
*Arenaria nuttallii*

**Plant:** A low, tufted perennial 5-15 cm tall.

**Flower:** 5 small (4-10 mm), white petals alternate with pink-tipped stamens.

**Leaves:** Linear to lance-shaped, pointed and hairy, 4-10 mm long, opposite one another along stems.

**Habitat:** Sagebrush hills to rocky terrain in high alpine zone.

**Range:** B.C. to California.

25

# TWIN-FLOWER

*Linnaea borealis*

**Plant:** A low, spreading, matted perennial with paired flowers on upright stalks to 10 cm tall.

**Flower:** 2 paired, pink, tubular flowers 10-17 mm long nod from an upright stem.

**Leaves:** Firm, ovate, dark green leaves 7-25 mm long are opposite one another and toothed at the tip.

**Habitat:** Open or dense forests and bogs, from lowlands to timberline.

**Range:** Alaska to California.

# ALASKA REIN-ORCHID

*Habenaria unalascensis*

**Plant:** Narrowly upright with leafless stems 10 to 80 cm tall.

**Flower:** Small (6-10 mm) green flowers are numerous along an upright stem, each with a 3-5 mm spur protruding backwards.

**Leaves:** 2 to 4 narrowly elliptic leaves near base of plant, 8-15 cm long.

**Habitat:** Dry to moist forests, meadows and streambanks at low to midelevations.

**Range:** Alaska to Baja California.

# PINESAP
*Hypopitys monotropa*

**Plant:** A low-growing, white to red perennial that nods at the tip, 5-25 cm tall.

**Flower:** 4 yellow to pink, hairy petals are 10-18 mm, flowers clustered in nodding heads.

**Leaves:** Small, bract-like elliptical leaves are pressed against the stem.

**Habitat:** In humus in coniferous forests at midelevations.

**Range:** B.C. to California.

**Note:** A non-photosynthetic saphrophyte.

# LADIES' TRESSES
*Spiranthes romanzoffiana*

**Plant:** A narrow, upright perennial 5-60 cm tall.

**Flower:** Small (8-18 mm long) white flowers are arranged in a distinctive, tight spiral on an erect stem.

**Leaves:** The several long, narrow leaves are nearly basal, 8-20 cm.

**Habitat:** Seeps, streambanks and bogs, low to midelevations.

**Range:** Alaska to California.

## RATTLESNAKE PLANTAIN
*Goodyera oblongifolia*

**Plant:** An evergreen perennial with a low rosette of leaves and upright flower stalk 10-40 cm tall.

**Flower:** Small (8-12 mm) dull white to greenish, hairy and hooded flowers are numerous along the erect stem.

**Leaves:** Oval leaves in a basal rosette, 3-8 cm long, dark green but mottled with white, especially on midvein.

**Habitat:** Dry to moist coniferous forests, low to subalpine.

**Range:** Alaska to Baja California.

ORCHIDACEAE · ORCHID FAMILY

## SLENDER BOG ORCHID
*Habenaria saccata*

**Plant:** A narrowly upright perennial 20-80 cm tall.

**Flower:** Small (6-20 mm) flowers are numerous along the erect stem, each with a bulbous spur protruding backwards.

**Leaves:** Oblong to elliptic, alternate up the stem, 4 to 16 cm long.

**Habitat:** Moist to boggy ground, low to high elevations.

**Range:** Alaska to California.

# WHITE HEATHER

*Cassiope mertensiana*

**Plant:** A spreading, matted evergreen shrub to 30 cm tall.

**Flower:** Fused petals form small (5-8 mm) white, drooping bells with reddish sepals, near branch tips.

**Leaves:** Very small (2-5 mm), scale-like leaves are arranged in 4 rows on stem.

**Habitat:** Subalpine to alpine meadows and subalpine forest edge.

**Range:** Alaska to California.

# ROUND-LEAVED SUNDEW

*Drosera rotundifolia*

**Plant:** A low-growing, tufted perennial of boggy ground, 5-25 cm tall.

**Flower:** 3-10 small white flowers, all on one side of stem, petals opening in sun only.

**Leaves:** In basal rosettes, the rounded blades 5-12 mm long, with red hairs topped by sticky glands.

**Habitat:** Sphagnum bogs, wet meadows from low to midelevations.

**Range:** Alaska to California.

**Note:** This plant is insectivorous, it obtains nutrients from small insects that get caught on the sticky leaves.

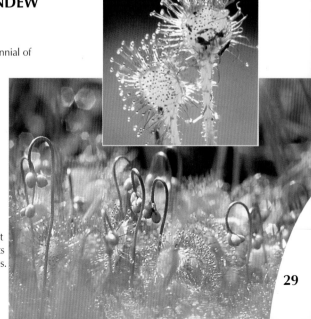

**29**

# WHITE RHODODENDRON
*Rhododendron albiflorum*

**Plant:** A branching shrub 1-2 m tall.

**Flower:** 5 fused white petals form a corolla 1.5-2 cm across, flowers in clusters of 2-4 along upper stem.

**Leaves:** Elliptic, shiny green leaves are 4-9 cm long, 8-20 mm wide, often appearing whorled or clustered together.

**Habitat:** Moist meadows, forests, stream-sides, mid- to subalpine elevations.

**Range:** B.C. to Oregon.

COMPOSITAE · COMPOSITE FAMILY

# WOOLLY PUSSYTOES
*Antennaria lanata*

**Plant:** A tufted, woolly perennial 10-20 cm tall.

**Flower:** Small (8-12 mm) whitish composite flowers are bunched together at stem tips in flat-topped to rounded heads.

**Leaves:** Basal leaves narrowly elliptic, gray-woolly, 3-10 cm long, stem leaves smaller.

**Habitat:** Moist meadows and ridges, sub-alpine to alpine.

**Range:** B.C. to Oregon.

**Note:** Woolly pussytoes is shown here growing with small-flowered paintbrush.

# ALPINE COLTSFOOT
*Petasites frigidus var. nivalis*

**Plant:** An upright perennial of wet places, to 40 cm tall, spreading from underground rhizomes.

**Flower:** White composite flowers are clumped together at the top of an erect, leafy stalk, male and female flowers on different plants.

**Leaves:** Mostly basal, long-stalked, 5-25 cm long, regularly lobed, woolly beneath.

**Habitat:** Wet meadows, seepage areas, stream and lake sides, subalpine to alpine.

**Range:** Alaska to California.

# TRAPPER'S TEA
*Ledum glandulosum*

**Plant:** A branching, evergreen shrub 1-2 m high.

**Flower:** Clusters of 5-30 white flowers, each about 1 cm across, forms at branch ends.

**Leaves:** Evergreen leaves are ovate-elliptic, 2-6 cm long, deep green above and whitish-hairy below.

**Habitat:** Bogs and moist coniferous forests, also among rocks above timberline.

**Range:** B.C. to California.

## NORTHERN BLACK CURRANT

*Ribes hudsonianum*

**Plant:** An erect, thornless shrub .5-3 m tall.

**Flower:** Many small (5-10 mm across), white flowers arranged in an elongated cluster along stalk.

**Fruit:** Unpalatable blue to black berries.

**Leaves:** Maple-like with 3-5 lobes and many teeth, 3-8 cm long, dotted with tiny yellow glands.

**Habitat:** Stream banks, moist woods at midelevations.

**Range:** Alaska to California.

**Note:** An alternative common name for this species is stinking currant.

## LYALL'S ANEMONE

*Anemone lyallii*

**Plant:** A delicate, upright perennial 8-20 cm tall.

**Flower:** No petals, but the 5-9 sepals are petal-like, 7-15 mm long, white to yellow, often tinged with blue, with 1-3 flowers per plant.

**Leaves:** 3 compound leaves, each with 3 leaflets, all attached at same point on stem.

**Habitat:** Open grasslands to deep forest and alpine ridges, especially near lakes and streams, coastal to midelevations.

**Range:** B.C. to California.

GROSSULARIACEAE · CURRANT FAMILY

# STINK CURRANT

*Ribes bracteosum*

**Plant:** An erect, ofen straggling, thornless shrub 1.5-3 m tall.

**Flower:** Small (7-10 mm wide), greenish-white flowers are arranged along a 10-30 cm long stalk.

**Fruit:** Black fruits are about 1 cm long and have a disagreeable taste.

**Leaves:** Maple-like leaves are deeply 5-7 lobed, toothed, 4-10 cm long, and are sprinkled with yellow, crystallline glands.

**Habitat:** Moist forests, streambanks.

**Range:** Alaska to California.

**Note:** The plant has a somewhat disagreeable odor.

GROSSULARIACEAE · CURRANT FAMILY

# STICKY CURRANT

*Ribes viscosissimum*

**Plant:** An erect to spreading, thornless shrub 1-2 m tall.

**Flower:** The white petals are 2.5-4 mm long, the flowers 6-10 mm wide, with 4-12 flowers in nodding clusters.

**Fruit:** Unpalatable, sticky blue to black berries.

**Leaves:** 3-6 cm wide, wider than long, 3-5 lobed, the lobes toothed but somewhat rounded at the tip.

**Habitat:** Along streams and on moist to rather dry forested slopes, from mid- to subalpine elevations.

**Range:** B.C. to California.

**33**

# YELLOW CORALROOT

*Corallorhiza trifida*

**Plant:** A rather delicate, narrowly erect, yellow-green perennial 10-25 cm tall.

**Flower:** 3-15 small (5-10 mm), white to greenish flowers spread along upper end of stalk.

**Leaves:** Reduced to sheathing bracts along the stem.

**Habitat:** Moist, shaded forests, midelevations to subalpine.

**Range:** Alaska to Oregon.

SAXIFRAGACEAE · SAXIFRAGE FAMILY

# BUTTERCUP-LEAVED SUKSDORFIA

*Suksdorfia ranunculifolia*

**Plant:** A small perennial with a cluster of basal leaves and a single flower stalk 10-30 cm tall.

**Flower:** Small (7-10 mm wide), white flowers with narrow petals clustered into a branching head at the top of a stalk.

**Leaf:** Basal leaves are 2-4 cm wide and somewhat wider than long, and are cleft into 3 toothed lobes, stem leaves are few and smaller than basal ones.

**Habitat:** On wet, mossy rock outcrops from low to subalpine zones.

**Range:** B.C. to California.

## SMALL WHITE VIOLET
*Viola macloskeyi*

**Plant:** A small perennial of wet ground, 3-6 cm high.

**Flower:** White with purplish lines on lower petal, 5-10 mm long, on a leafless stem.

**Leaves:** Ovate to cordate (heart-shaped), 3-6 cm long, the leaf stalks 2-4 cm long.

**Habitat:** Boggy or wet ground in mountain forest to alpine zones.

**Range:** Alaska to California.

## STICKY TOFIELDIA
*Tofieldia glutinosa*

**Plant:** A grass-like, erect, sticky perennial 10-50 cm tall.

**Flower:** The six white tepals are 3-5.5 mm long, the anthers purple, many flowers clustered tightly together at the end of an upright, sticky stalk.

**Leaves:** The sheathing, grass-like leaves are mostly basal and 5-15 cm long.

**Habitat:** Wet meadows, bogs, seepages, and streambanks from low to subalpine zones.

**Range:** Alaska to California.

# CUT-LEAVED DAISY
*Erigeron compositus*

**Plant:** A low, tufted perennial 3-25 cm tall.

**Flower:** White to pink ray flowers (petals) 5-10 mm long, the center yellow, one composite flower head per stalk.

**Leaves:** Nearly all basal, small and finely once or twice divided into narrow segments, the final segments 2-6 mm long.

**Habitat:** Sandy and rocky places, from low to high elevations.

**Range:** Alaska to California.

# BEARGRASS
*Xerophyllum temax*

**Plant:** A tufted, grass-like, evergreen perennial with flower stalks .5-1.5 m tall.

**Flower:** Hundreds of small (1 cm wide) white flowers crowded together in a cone 10-50 cm long at the top of upright stalk.

**Leaves:** Basal leaves in large clumps, tough and wiry, 15-60 cm long, stem leaves progressively shorter.

**Habitat:** Open woods and clearings, from low elevations to subalpine.

**Range:** B.C. to California.

# WHITE BOG-ORCHID

*Habenaria dilatata*

**Plant:** A narrow, upright perennial 10-80 cm tall.

**Flower:** Many showy white flowers 1-2 cm long on an erect stem, each flower with a narrow spur projecting backwards.

**Leaves:** Attached to and sheathing the erect flower stem, elliptical, the largest 4-15 cm long and 1-3 cm wide, smaller above.

**Habitat:** Bogs, seepages, moist meadows from lowlands to subalpine.

**Range:** Alaska to California.

# LEAFY MITREWORT

*Mitella caulescens*

**Plant:** A narrow, upright perennial 20-40 cm tall.

**Flower:** 10-25 small (5-9 mm wide) white flowers along upright stem, the delicate petals divided into thread-like segments.

**Leaves:** Basal leaves 3-5 lobed and notched at stem, 3-7 cm wide, the few stem leaves smaller.

**Habitat:** Moist, shaded forests and wet meadows at low to midelevations.

**Range:** B.C. to California.

37

## MOUNTAIN-AVENS
*Dryas octopetala*

**Plant:** A low, matted, evergreen perennial, the flower stems 3-15 cm tall.

**Flower:** 8-12 cream-white petals, each 10-12 mm long, surround a yellow eye, each flower is solitary on a stem.

**Fruits:** Seeds have feathery plumes attached that together form a fluffy mass.

**Leaves:** Leathery, elliptical, dark green leaves are 1-3 cm long, and coarsely toothed.

**Habitat:** Gravel bars, rocky sites, ridges, from midelevations to alpine.

**Range:** Alaska to Oregon.

## UTAH HONEYSUCKLE
*Lonicera utahensis*

**Plant:** An often somewhat straggling shrub 1-2 m tall.

**Flower:** Creamy-white flowers, each 1-2 cm long, are tubular and occur in pairs.

**Fruit:** Bright red berries are about 1 cm thick and occur in pairs.

**Leaves:** Elliptic to oblong, 2-8 cm long, opposite one another on stem.

**Habitat:** Moist forests, streamsides, thickets from mid- to subalpine zones.

**Range:** B.C. to California.

38

# SMALL-FLOWERED PAINTBRUSH

*Castilleja parviflora*

**Plant:** An upright, unbranched perennial 15-30 cm tall, often with several adjacent flower stems.

**Flower:** Color can be white or red, what appear to be the petals in all paintbrushes are actually bracts around the flower, these bracts are 12-25 mm long in this species.

**Leaves:** 1-4 cm long, cleft into several deep lobes, the central lobe the widest.

**Habitat:** Subalpine meadows and high elevation stream banks.

**Range:** Alaska to Oregon.

# NARROW-LEAFED OWL CLOVER

*Orthocarpus attenuata*

**Plant:** A narrow, unbranched, erect perennial 10-35 cm tall.

**Flower:** The colored bracts around the flowers are white, yellow or purple, the protruding corollas (fused petals) white or pinkish, flowers crowded together at top of stem.

**Leaves:** 2-6 cm long and very narrow, the upper ones sometimes with several narrow lobes.

**Habitat:** Open, grassy slopes and meadows from low to midelevations.

**Range:** B.C. to California.

39

# PYGMY LEWISIA

*Lewisia pygmaea*

**Plant:** A diminutive perennial 2-8 cm tall.

**Flower:** 1 flower per stem, each with 5-9 white to pink petals, 6-17 mm long, the 2 sepals per flower are characteristic of the Purslane Family.

**Leaves:** Several rather succulent, linear, basal leaves in a tuft, 5-15 cm long and 1-6 mm wide.

**Habitat:** Open rocky and gravelly areas, subalpine to alpine.

**Range:** Washington to California.

# TUFTED SAXIFRAGE

*Saxifraga caespitosa*

**Plant:** A small, mat-forming perennial with several erect stems 3-15 cm tall.

**Flower:** Small cluster of flowers at end of upright stems, each with 5 white or yellowish petals 3-8 mm long.

**Leaves:** Small and mostly basal, 5-20 mm long, cleft into 3 lobes.

**Habitat:** Cliffs, talus and rocky slopes from sea level to arctic alpine.

**Range:** Alaska to Oregon.

# ALPINE ANEMONE

*Anemone drummondii*

**Plant:** An upright perennial 10-25 cm tall.

**Flower:** No petals, but sepals petal-like, white or tinged with blue, 6-9 in number, each 10-20 mm long.

**Fruit:** The numerous seeds have fine hairs attached, forming a silky seed head.

**Leaves:** Mostly basal, on long stalks, the blade 2 or 3 times divided into fine leaflets, also 2 stemless leaves opposite one another below the flower.

**Habitat:** Rocky ridges and slopes, subalpine to alpine.

**Range:** Alaska to California.

# ELMERA

*Elmera racemosa*

**Plant:** An upright to spreading perennial 10-25 cm tall.

**Flower:** Calyx (fused sepals) yellowish, 6-9 mm long, the tiny white petals divided into 3-7 lobes, 10-30 flowers at upper end of stem.

**Leaves:** Kidney-shaped, 3-5 cm wide, wider than long, toothed, basal leaves on long stalks.

**Habitat:** Rocky ledges and talus slopes, subalpine and alpine.

**Range:** Washington.

41

## GOOSEFOOT VIOLET

*Viola purpurea*

**Plant:** A perennial 5-15 mm tall.

**Flower:** 5-12 mm long, petals yellow with brown pencilling (lines).

**Leaves:** Fleshy, arrowhead-shaped blades with rounded teeth, often with purple veins, 2-5 cm in length, on long stalks.

**Habitat:** Open ridges and slopes, low to high elevations.

**Range:** Washington to California.

## BOG ST. JOHN'S-WORT

*Hypericum anagalloides*

**Plant:** A low, mat-forming perennial with upright flower stems 3-15 cm tall.

**Flower:** 5 yellow petals 3-5 mm long, the flowers 8-12 mm wide, on upright or creeping stems.

**Leaves:** Elliptical and opposite one another on stem, 5-15 mm long.

**Habitat:** Wet meadows, seepages, bogs, from low to montane elevations.

**Range:** B.C. to Baja California.

# MOUNTAIN MONKEYFLOWER

*Mimulus tilingii*

**Plant:** An erect to spreading perennial 5-20 cm tall.

**Flower:** Bright yellow, 2-4 cm long, solitary or few (2-5) per stem.

**Leaves:** Ovate and toothed, 1-2.5 cm long, opposite one another on stem.

**Habitat:** Along streams and in seepages at subalpine and alpine elevations.

**Range:** B.C. to Baja California.

# SPREADING STONECROP

*Sedum divergens*

**Plant:** A creeping, mat-forming succulent with upright stems 5-15 cm tall.

**Flower:** 5 bright yellow petals 7-9 mm long, flowers 5-15 together at stem tips.

**Leaves:** Small (4-8 mm), thick and fleshy, green to bright red, opposite one another on the stem.

**Habitat:** Rock cliffs, ledges, scree slopes from low to alpine elevations.

**Range:** B.C. to Oregon.

# SILVERBACK LUINA

*Luina hypoleuca*

**Plant:** A branching perennial from a woody base, 15-40 cm tall.

**Flower:** Small (5-8 mm) composite flowers with white to yellow disk flowers only, no ray flowers (no petals), 10-20 composite heads blooming together in a flat-topped cluster.

**Leaves:** Stemless, elliptical, 3-6 cm long and 1-3 cm wide, white-hairy on the underside.

**Habitat:** Open rocky slopes and cliff crevices, mid- to subalpine elevations.

**Range:** B.C. to California.

# SILVERCROWN LUINA

*Luina nardosmia*

**Plant:** An upright perennial 40-90 cm tall.

**Flower:** Composite flowers with yellow disk flowers only, no ray flowers (no petals), 5-10 of these clustered in an elongate head.

**Leaves:** Large, 15-20 cm long and 20-35 cm wide, mostly basal, circular in outline but deeply cleft into separate lobes.

**Habitat:** Dry meadows and open forests at rather low elevations.

**Range:** Washington to Oregon.

# SHRUBBY CINQUEFOIL
*Potentilla fruiticosa*

**Plant:** An erect to spreading shrub 10-100 cm tall.

**Flower:** 5 bright yellow petals 8-13 mm long, flowers solitary or 3-7 together.

**Leaves:** Pinnately compound, with 5 narrow leaflets 10-20 mm long.

**Habitat:** In varied, open habitats, from the seashore to alpine ridges.

**Range:** Alaska to California.

# VILLOUS CINQUEFOIL
*Potentilla villosa*

**Plant:** A low-growing, gray-hairy perennial.

**Flower:** Five petals, each notched at the tip, 5-8 mm long, flowers 1 to several on stems 3-20 cm tall.

**Leaves:** Palmately compound, with three villous (long-hairy), toothed leaflets, each .5-1.5 cm long.

**Habitat:** Typically on alpine talus slopes, but on rocks near the ocean on Vancouver Island.

**Range:** Alaska to Oregon.

# YELLOW AVALANCHE LILY, GLACIER LILY

*Erythronium grandiflorum*

**Plant:** A perennial 10-30 cm tall, blooming soon after the snow melts.
**Flower:** 6 yellow tepals 25-35 cm long, all swept backwards, with large yellow to red anthers protruding forward.
**Leaves:** 2-3 basal, elliptical leaves, 10-20 cm long.
**Habitat:** Sagebrush slopes to alpine elevations, in sunny habitats.
**Range:** B.C. to Oregon.

# PRIMROSE MONKEYFLOWER

*Mimulus primuloides*

**Plant:** A low, matted perennial 5-20 cm tall.
**Flower:** Corolla (the fused petals) yellow with red dots, 1-2 cm long.
**Leaves:** Basal, oblanceolate, 7-25 mm long and 3-10 mm wide.
**Habitat:** Wet meadows and bogs, from moderate to alpine elevations.
**Range:** Washington to California.

# YELLOW MONKEYFLOWER

*Mimulus guttatus*

**Plant:** Small and annual (2-10 cm tall) or larger and perennial (up to 1 m).

**Flower:** 1-4 cm long in the perennial form, red spotted inside the fused petals, the upper calyx tooth longer than the others, several to many flowers per stem.

**Leaves:** Ovate and sharply toothed, 5-40 cm long, opposite one another on the stem.

**Habitat:** In wet places, from sea level to the subalpine zone.

**Range:** Alaska to Baja California.

# GOLDEN FLEABANE

*Erigeron aureus*

**Plant:** A low-growing perennial 2-15 cm tall.

**Flower:** One composite flower head per plant, with numerous ray flowers (petals) 6-9 mm long, and a green to yellow center.

**Leaves:** The mostly basal leaves are 1-2 cm long, elliptical to rounded, on stalks about as long as the leaf blades.

**Habitat:** Rocky places at high elevations.

**Range:** B.C. to Washington.

# DWARF HAWKSBEARD

*Crepis nana*

**Plant:** A glaucous (powdery blue-green) perennial typically 5-10 cm tall.

**Flower:** Composite heads with 9-12 yellow ray flowers (petals) 1-2 cm long, with 1-10 heads on a stem, often in among leaves.

**Leaves:** Mostly basal, elliptical to arrowhead-shaped, 1-4 cm long.

**Habitat:** Talus slopes and other open stony ground at subalpine and alpine elevations.

**Range:** Alaska to California.

# YELLOW MOUNTAIN HEATHER

*Phyllodoce glanduliflora*

**Plant:** A low, spreading, evergreen shrub with erect stems 10-40 cm tall.

**Flower:** Corolla (fused petals) dirty yellow to greenish white, 5-7 mm long, wider at the base and narrowed at the tip.

**Leaves:** Narrow and evergreen, 6-12 mm long, alternate on the stem.

**Habitat:** Alpine and subalpine meadows.

**Range:** Alaska to Oregon.

# MOUNTAIN BUTTERCUP

*Ranunculus eschscholtzii*

**Plant:** A tufted perennial 10-20 cm tall.

**Flower:** 5 shiny yellow petals 7-15 mm long, typically indented at the rounded tip, with 1-3 flowers per stem.

**Leaves:** The primarily basal leaves are 1-3 cm long, and typically cleft into 3-5 segments which are again divided into 3 lobes.

**Habitat:** Wet meadows and rocky seeps at moderate to high elevations.

**Range:** Alaska to California.

# PAYSON'S DRABA

*Draba paysonii*

**Plant:** A low, matted, perennial 1-3 cm tall.

**Flower:** The 4 bright yellow petals are only 2.5-4 mm long, with 3-10 flowers at the top of a 1-3 cm tall stalk.

**Leaves:** Narrow and hairy, 4-14 mm long, with a prominant midrib, somewhat curled when dry.

**Habitat:** Rocky places, subalpine to alpine.

**Range:** B.C. to California.

49

# NORTHERN GOLDENROD

*Solidago multiradiata*

**Plant:** An erect to leaning perennial 5-50 cm tall.

**Flower:** Composite heads with both yellow ray and disk flowers, the rays 4-8 mm long, with several to many heads at top of stem.

**Leaves:** Basal leaves typically oblanceolate and somewhat toothed, 2-10 cm long, the stem leaves smaller.

**Habitat:** Dry open forests, wet meadows, and rocky ridges from mid- to high elevations.

**Range:** Alaska to California.

ROSACEAE · ROSE FAMILY

# SIBBALDIA

*Sibbaldia procumbens*

**Plant:** A low, mat-forming perennial, the flower stalks 3-8 cm tall.

**Flower:** The 5 yellow-green sepals, 2-4 mm in length, are longer than the small, narrow petals, 1 to several flowers per erect stem.

**Leaves:** Small, compound leaves are divided in three wedge-shaped leaflets that are toothed at the tip, each leaflet 1-2 cm long.

**Habitat:** Open gravelly areas and rocky ridges from mid- to alpine elevations.

**Range:** Alaska to California.

CRASSULACEAE · STONECROP FAMILY

# LANCE-LEAVED STONECROP

*Sedum lanceolatum*

**Plant:** A mat-forming, succulent perennial with flower stems 5-25 cm tall.

**Flower:** The 5 yellow petals are lanceolate and pointed at the tip, with 5-30 flowers in a flat-topped cluster at stem tips.

**Leaves:** Lanceolate, fleshy-thickened, 5-20 mm long, most falling off as the plant blooms.

**Habitat:** Open, rocky places from low to subalpine elevations.

**Range:** Alaska to California.

VIOLACEAE · VIOLET FAMILY

# ROUND-LEAVED YELLOW VIOLET

*Viola orbiculata*

**Plant:** A low, tufted perennial 2.5-6 cm tall.

**Flower:** Yellow flowers are 5-15 mm long, with purple pencilling (lines) on the lower 3 petals.

**Leaves:** The mainly basal leaves are rounded (orbicular), 2-4 cm wide, shallowly toothed, and are on long stems.

**Habitat:** Moist mountain forests to subalpine meadows.

**Range:** B.C. to Oregon.

## SAXIFRAGACEAE · SAXIFRAGE FAMILY

# ALPINE MITREWORT
*Mitella pentandra*

**Plant:** A tufted perennial 15-30 cm tall.

**Flower:** The sepals are fused into a cup-shaped calyx, from which the delicate 2-3 mm long thread-like petals emerge.

**Leaves:** All basal, 2-8 cm long, ovate, lobed and toothed, notched at stem, on long stalks.

**Habitat:** Moist woods, streamsides, wet meadows from mid- to subalpine zones.

**Range:** Alaska to California.

## SCROPHULARIACEAE · FIGWORT FAMILY

# COILED-BEAK LOUSEWORT
*Pedicularis contorta*

**Plant:** An erect perennial with 1 to several stems 15-60 cm tall.

**Flower:** Corolla (fused petals) white to yellow, about 1 cm long, the upper petal curved and twisted, flowers numerous along upper stem.

**Leaves:** Basal and on the stem, pinnately compound, the leaflets finely toothed and fern-like.

**Habitat:** Open forests and meadows at mid to alpine elevations.

**Range:** B.C. to California.

# BRACTED LOUSEWORT

*Pedicularis bracteosa*

**Plant:** An erect, unbranched perennial 20-100 cm tall.

**Flower:** Corolla (fused petals) purple to red or yellow, the upper petal forming a hood, the many flowers crowded together in an elongated head at the top of the erect stem.

**Leaves:** Pinnately compound and fern-like, the leaflets narrow and finely toothed.

**Habitat:** Moist open forests, meadows, clearings from mid- to alpine elevations.

**Range:** B.C. to California.

# YELLOW WILLOWHERB

*Epilobium luteum*

**Plant:** An upright to sprawling perennial 20-70 cm tall, sometimes forming colonies of plants due to spreading rhizomes.

**Flower:** 4 yellow petals are 14-18 mm long, notched at the tip, with 2-10 flowers near tip of stem.

**Leaves:** Elliptical and serrate, 3-8 cm long, opposite one another on stem.

**Habitat:** Along streams and in seepage areas, from mid- to subalpine elevations.

**Range:** Alaska to Oregon.

# HEART-LEAVED ARNICA

*Arnica cordifolia*

**Plant:** A perennial 10-50 cm tall, sometimes forming extensive colonies from underground rhizomes.

**Flower:** A yellow composite flower, the rays (petals) 10-15 in number and 1.5-3 cm long, with 1-3 heads per stalk.

**Leaves:** Ovate and serrate, the basal leaves indented at the stalk (heart-shaped), 3-9 cm long, stem leaves opposite one another.

**Habitat:** Mostly in coniferous woodlands, at low to midelevations.

**Range:** Alaska to California.

# HAIRY ARNICA

*Arnica mollis*

**Plant:** An upright perennial 15-60 cm tall.

**Flower:** A yellow composite flower, the rays (petals) 12-18 in number and 1.5-2.5 cm long, with 1-3 heads per stalk.

**Leaves:** Basal leaves elliptic to oblong, 3-10 cm long, tapered to the stem (not indented), stem leaves opposite one another.

**Habitat:** Moist meadows and forests from mid- to alpine elevations.

**Range:** B.C. to California.

54

# MOUNTAIN ARNICA

*Arnica latifolia*

**Plant:** An erect perennial with several pairs of leaves opposite one another on the stem, 10-60 cm tall.

**Flower:** A yellow composite flower, the rays (petals) 8-13 in number and 1.5-3 cm long, with 1-3 heads per stalk.

**Leaves:** Ovate and serrate, the basal leaves not or barely indented at the stalk, 4-14 cm long, stem leaves opposite one another.

**Habitat:** Moist, open forests, streamsides, meadows at mid- to high elevations.

**Range:** Alaska to California.

# COPPERBUSH

*Cladothamnus pyroliflorus*

**Plant:** A shrub 1.5-3 m tall, with loose, shredding copper colored bark.

**Flower:** Solitary at stem tips, 5 spreading red to copper-colored petals 10-15 mm long, and a stout, curved style.

**Leaves:** Elliptic to oblanceolate with a small point at tip, 2-5 cm long, somewhat glaucous (covered with a fine, waxy-gray powder).

**Habitat:** Moist forests, stream banks, bog edges in subalpine zone.

**Range:** Alaska to Oregon.

## FEW-FLOWERED DESERT PARSLEY

*Lomatium martindalei*

**Plant:** A tufted perennial 5-15 mm tall.

**Flower:** Tiny (2-3 mm wide) individual flowers are white to yellowish, and are gathered together in several heads 3-8 cm wide.

**Leaves:** All basal, pinnately compound, the leaflets finely divided and parsley-like.

**Habitat:** Rock outcrops and ridges in subapline to alpine zones.

**Range:** B.C. to Oregon.

## HOUNDS TONGUE HAWKWEED

*Hieracium cynoglossoides*

**Plant:** An erect perennial with a single stem, 20-100 cm tall.

**Flower:** Numerous yellow ray flowers (petals) in each composite head, the rays 1-1.5 cm long, heads 2-15 at top of stem.

**Leaves:** Elliptic and elongate, 5-25 cm long, shorter up the stem, stiffly hairy.

**Habitat:** Dry open places at low to moderate elevations.

**Range:** B.C. to Oregon.

# FIELD LOCOWEED
*Oxytropis campestris*

**Plant:** A tufted perennial 5-25 cm tall.

**Flower:** Cream to yellow flowers are 10-20 mm long, in tight clusters at the end of leafless stems.

**Leaves:** All basal, 3-20 cm long, pinnately compound with 5-41 elliptical leaflets which are 5-30 mm long.

**Habitat:** Exposed, rocky terrain in subalpine to alpine zones.

**Range:** Alaska to Washington.

# LYALL'S GOLDENWEED
*Haplopappus lyallii*

**Plant:** A small, sticky perennial with flower stems 3-15 cm tall.

**Flower:** Composite heads 2-3 cm wide, with yellow ray and disk flowers, solitary on upright stems.

**Leaves:** Oblanceolate, 1-5 cm long and 1-5 mm wide.

**Habitat:** Scree slopes and rocky ridges in the alpine zone.

**Range:** B.C. to Oregon.

## ELMER'S BUTTERWEED

*Senecio elmeri*

**Plant:** A tufted perennial 10-30 cm tall.

**Flower:** Yellow composite heads, the ray flowers 8-16 mm long, 2-10 heads per stem, some often nodding.

**Leaves:** Oblanceolate, 5-20 cm tall, shiny green and coarsely toothed.

**Habitat:** Moist scree and talus slopes, subalpine to alpine.

**Range:** B.C. to Washington.

## DWARF HULSEA

*Hulsea nana*

**Plant:** A low, tufted, hairy plant 4-15 cm tall.

**Flower:** Yellow composite heads solitary at end of stems, the ray flowers (petals) 6-15 mm long.

**Leaves:** Oblanceolate and deeply toothed, 3-6 cm long, crowded near base of plant.

**Habitat:** At high elevations on volcanic cinder cones, pumice plains, and moraines.

**Range:** Washington to California.

# TIGER LILY

*Lilium columbianum*

**Plant:** An upright perennial 60-120 cm tall.

**Flower:** 6 orange tepals 4-6 cm long, sharply recurved and brown-spotted, with large yellow to brown anthers protruding forward, 2-20 flowers per stem.

**Leaves:** Elliptic, 4-10 cm long, whorled or alternate on stem.

**Habitat:** Lowlands to montane meadows, in open forests, thickets and clearings.

**Range:** B.C. to California.

# ORANGE AGOSERIS

*Agoseris aurantiaca*

**Plant:** A narrowly erect perennial, the flower stalk 10-60 cm tall.

**Flower:** A composite head composed of orange ray flowers, the rays 1-2 cm long and toothed at the tip.

**Leaves:** All basal, long and narrow, 5-30 cm long and 5-30 mm wide, sometimes with a few teeth or lobes.

**Habitat:** Moist to dry meadows, forest openings, from low to high elevations.

**Range:** B.C. to California.

59

# INDIAN PAINTBRUSH
*Castilleja miniata*

**Plant:** A perennial with clustered stems, 20-80 cm tall.

**Flower:** Bracts around corolla red, corolla 20-40 mm long, flowers clustered in tight heads at end of stems.

**Leaves:** Lanceolate, 2-7 cm long, most leaves unlobed, alternate on stem.

**Habitat:** Open meadows, grassy hillsides, stream banks, and lake margins, low to subalpine elevations.

**Range:** Alaska to California.

# ALPINE PAINTBRUSH
*Castilleja rhexifolia*

**Plant:** A perennial with clustered stems, 10-30 cm tall.

**Flower:** Bracts around flowers crimson to scarlet, corolla 20-35 mm long, protruding beyond bracts, flowers clustered in tight heads at end of stems.

**Leaves:** Narrowly elliptic and usually without lobes, 1-5 cm long, alternate on stem.

**Habitat:** Alpine and subalpine meadows and rocky ridges.

**Range:** B.C. to Oregon.

# HARSH PAINTBRUSH

*Castilleja hispida*

**Plant:** An erect perennial with clustered stems 20-60 cm tall, the plant conspicuously hairy.

**Flower:** Bracts around the corolla red, the corolla 20-40 mm long, flowers clustered in tight heads at end of stems.

**Leaves:** Oblong, 2-6 cm long, with 1-3 pairs of narrow lobes.

**Habitat:** Meadows and forest openings, from low to subalpine elevations.

**Range:** B.C. to Oregon.

# MOUNTAIN SORREL

*Oxyria digyna*

**Plant:** A tufted perennial 5-40 cm tall, often tinged red.

**Flower:** Very small (1.5 mm), yellow to red, with many flowers densely clustered on upright stems.

**Leaves:** Basal with long stalks and broad, heart-shaped blades 1-5 cm wide.

**Habitat:** On rocky slopes and ledges at subalpine to alpine elevations.

**Range:** Alaska to California.

**Note:** The leaves are sour but edible.

# ROCK PENSTEMON

*Penstemon rupicola*

**Plant:** A matted, woody-based perennial 5-10 cm tall.

**Flower:** Pink to red, 25-36 mm long, usually 2-6 blooming together at tip of stems.

**Leaves:** Round to ovate, thick and firm, 8-18 mm long and nearly as wide, some serrate.

**Habitat:** On cliffs, ledges and rocky slopes, low to high elevations.

**Range:** Washington to California.

# RED COLUMBINE

*Aquilegia formosa*

**Plant:** An upright, branching perennial 15-100 cm tall.

**Flower:** 5 flaring red petal-like sepals 15-25 mm long, 5 red spurs point backward, and numerous yellow stamens protruding forward.

**Leaves:** Palmately compound, the 3 leaflets again divided in 3, these toothed and lobed.

**Habitat:** Moist lowland forests to subalpine meadows.

**Range:** Alaska to Baja California.

# PINK MONKEYFLOWER
*Mimulus lewisii*

**Plant:** A robust, erect, multi-stemmed perennial 30-100 cm tall.

**Flower:** Pink-purple and marked with yellow, 3-5.5 cm long, on long stalks extending from leaf axils.

**Leaves:** Elliptic and serrate, 3-7 cm long, opposite one another on stem, generally viscid (slippery).

**Habitat:** Along streams and other wet places, from sea level to midelevations.

**Range:** B.C. to California.

# CANDYSTICK
*Allotropa virgata*

**Plant:** A narrowly erect perennial with a red and white striped stem, 10-40 cm tall.

**Flower:** Many small (5 mm) white to red petalless flowers arranged along upright stem.

**Leaves:** Reduced to lanceolate bracts on the lower stem.

**Habitat:** In humus of coniferous forests from low to midelevations.

**Range:** B.C. to California.

**Note:** This species is a saprophyte, it gets its carbohydrates from organic matter in the soil rather than from photosynthesis.

# PRINCE'S PINE, PIPSISSEWA

*Chimaphila umbellata*

**Plant:** A low, erect, evergreen shrub 10-30 cm tall.

**Flower:** 5 spreading pink petals 5-7 mm long, with 5-15 downward facing flowers at tip of upright stem.

**Leaves:** In whorls, narrowly elliptical, 3-7 cm long, leathery and sharply toothed.

**Habitat:** In coniferous forests, at low to midelevations.

**Range:** Alaska to California.

# PINK WINTERGREEN

*Pyrola asarifolia*

**Plant:** A rhizomatous, spreading perennial, the flower stems 15-40 cm tall.

**Flower:** 5 pink to purple petals 5-7 mm long, with 10-25 downward facing flowers arranged along the upper portion of a red stem.

**Leaves:** All basal, heart-shaped, leathery and shiny, 3-8 cm long.

**Habitat:** Moist forests, thickets, meadows from low to subalpine elevations.

**Range:** Alaska to California.

# WESTERN CORALROOT

*Corallorhiza mertensiana*

**Plant:** A narrowly erect perennial 15-40 cm tall.

**Flower:** Delicate pink flowers 15-20 mm wide, 15-30 flowers loosely arranged along upright stem.

**Leaves:** Reduced to sheathing bracts the same color as stem.

**Habitat:** In moist coniferous forests at midelevations.

**Range:** Alaska to California.

# MOUNTAIN BELLS

*Stenanthium occidentale*

**Plant:** A narrow, upright perennial 10-40 cm tall.

**Flower:** Yellow to purple, 8-15 mm long, the tepals curved backwards, 5-15 flowers along upper stem.

**Leaves:** Few and all basal, grass-like, 15-30 cm long.

**Habitat:** Rocky faces and seepages, moist meadows, normally subalpine, occasionally at lower elevations.

**Range:** B.C. to California.

# RED WILLOWHERB
*Epilobium latifolium*

**Plant:** An upright to straggling perennial 5-40 cm tall.

**Flower:** 4 rose-purple petals 15-25 mm long, sepals also colored, 3-12 flowers near stem tip.

**Leaves:** Ovate to lanceolate, 3-8 cm long, opposite below and alternate above, often grayish.

**Habitat:** Sandy, gravel soils on river bars, stream banks, and cliffs, mid- to high elevation.

**Range:** Alaska to California.

# ALPINE WILLOWHERB
*Epilobium alpinum*

**Plant:** A low, tufted to matted perennial 5-30 cm tall.

**Flower:** 4 pink or white petals, 3-13 mm long, deeply notched at the tip, 1 to several flowers blooming at stem tips.

**Leaves:** Elliptical, 1-5 cm long, opposite one another on stem.

**Habitat:** Moist banks, meadows, seepages, and streambanks in subalpine and alpine zones.

**Range:** Alaska to California.

# MOSS CAMPION
*Silene acaulis*

**Plant:** A matted cushion 2-6 cm tall and as much as 200 cm wide.

**Flower:** 5 pink to lavender petals, notched at the tip, flowers about 1 cm across.

**Leaves:** Basal, linear, 4-10 mm long and about 1 mm wide.

**Habitat:** Rocky ridges, crevices, scree slopes in alpine zone.

**Range:** Alaska to Oregon.

# MOUNTAIN SPIREA
*Spiraea densiflora*

**Plant:** A spreading to erect shrub .5-1 m tall.

**Flower:** Flowers very small (5 mm wide), pink, many gathered together in dense, flat-topped clusters.

**Leaves:** Elliptical and serrate, 2-4 cm long, alternate on stem.

**Habitat:** Along streams and lakes, in forests and clearings from sea level to subalpine.

**Range:** B.C. to California.

# CASCADE BLUEBERRY

*Vaccinium deliciosum*

**Plant:** A low, matted shrub 5-40 cm tall.

**Flower:** Pink, round flowers are 6-7 mm long and solitary in leaf axils.

**Leaves:** Elliptical, 1.5-5 cm long, alternate on the stem, whitish below.

**Habitat:** Subalpine meadows, alpine ridges.

**Range:** B.C. to Oregon.

**Note:** One of the tastiest of the blueberry species.

# MOUNTAIN BOXWOOD

*Pachistima myrsinites*

**Plant:** An upright, branching shrub 20-60 cm tall.

**Flower:** Tiny (3-4 mm wide) maroon flowers are hidden the leaf axils.

**Leaves:** Elliptical, glossy, leathery, serrate, 1-3 cm long, opposite one another on stem.

**Habitat:** Coniferous forests and open mountain slopes, low to midelevations.

**Range:** B.C. to California.

# ROSY TWISTEDSTALK
*Streptopus roseus*

**Plant:** An upright, simple or branched perennial 15-30 cm tall.

**Flower:** White to rose colored, bell-shaped with 6 tepals, 6-10 mm long, 1 or 2 flowers under each upper leaf, on curving stalks.

**Leaves:** Broadly elliptic and parallel veined, 5-9 cm long, alternate up the stem.

**Habitat:** Moist coniferous forests, stream banks, and moist clearings from low to subalpine elevations.

**Range:** Alaska to Oregon.

# FOOL'S HUCKLEBERRY
*Menziesia ferruginea*

**Plant:** A straggling shrub .5-2 m tall.

**Flower:** Corolla (fused petals) yellow-red, 6-8 mm long, on hairy stalks 1-2 cm long, with 1-5 flowers growing from branch junctions.

**Leaves:** Ovate elliptic, 4-6 cm long, alternate on stem or appearing whorled, skunky aroma when crushed.

**Habitat:** Moist forests, from low to subalpine elevations

**Range:** B.C. to Oregon.

**Note:** Easily mistaken for Cascade azalea or a blueberry/huckleberry species.

## LEIBERG'S FLEABANE
*Erigeron leibergii*

**Plant:** A somewhat scraggly perennial 5-25 cm high.

**Flower:** A composite with blue to pink ray flowers (petals) 5-12 mm long and yellow disk flowers.

**Leaves:** Basal leaves oblanceolate, 4-12 cm long, stem leaves elliptical and smaller.

**Habitat:** Cliffs, rocky slopes, and ridges from subalpine to alpine.

**Range:** Washington.

## ALPINE ASTER
*Aster alpigenus*

**Plant:** An upright perennial 3-40 cm tall with flowers solitary on stems.

**Flower:** A composite with violet ray flowers 7-15 mm long and yellow disk flowers.

**Leaves:** Basal leaves linear to oblanceolate, 2-25 cm long, stem leaves much reduced.

**Habitat:** Mountain meadows, subalpine to alpine.

**Range:** Washington to California.

# LEAFY ASTER

*Aster foliaceus*

**Plant:** An upright perennial, variable in height and growth pattern, 10-60 cm tall.

**Flower:** A composite with blue to rose ray flowers (petals) 1-2 cm long and yellow disk flowers, at least a few of the bracts just below the flowers are usually slightly enlarged and leaf-like.

**Leaves:** Oblanceolate below, 5-12 mm long, lanceolate and smaller above.

**Habitat:** Sandy, gravel soils on river bars and stream banks, moist mountain meadows and forest openings.

**Range:** Alaska to California.

# SUBALPINE DAISY

*Erigeron perigrinus*

**Plant:** A upright perennial 10-70 cm tall.

**Flower:** A composite head with 30-80 pink to lavender ray flowers 8-25 mm long and yellow disk flowers.

**Leaves:** Basal leaves oblanceolate, 3-9 cm long, progressively reduced in size up the stem.

**Habitat:** Moist meadows, streamsides and open forests from mid- to high elevations.

**Range:** Alaska to California.

## MAPLE-LEAF CURRANT
*Ribes howellii*

**Plant:** A spreading to erect, non-spiny shrub .5-1 m tall.

**Flower:** 5 spreading red petals 1-1.5 mm long, with 7-12 flowers loosely clustered on a drooping stalk attached in the leaf axils.

**Fruit:** Unpalatable blue to black berries, 1 cm thick.

**Leaves:** Mapleleaf-like, with 3-7 lobes and serrate edges, 3-8 cm wide.

**Habitat:** Montane to alpine stream banks, thickets and open ridges and rock slides.

**Range:** B.C. to Oregon.

GROSSULARIACEAE · CURRANT FAMILY

## SWAMP GOOSEBERRY, BLACK GOOSEBERRY
*Ribes lacustre*

**Plant:** A sprawling shrub with many spines on the stem and larger spines at leaf nodes, 1-2 m tall.

**Flower:** Tiny flowers, with sepals longer than petals, the sepals pale pink to red, 2.5-3 mm long, with 7-15 flowers arranged along a drooping stalk.

**Leaves:** Mapleleaf-like, with 3-7 lobes and serrate edges, 2-5 cm wide, shiny green.

**Habitat:** Moist forests and stream banks from lowlands to subalpine.

**Range:** Alaska to California.

# ELEPHANT'S HEAD

*Pedicularis groenlandica*

**Plant:** A tufted perennial with an erect flower stalk 10-60 cm tall.

**Flower:** Numerous pink-purple flowers along an upright stalk, each with a narrowed, twisted petal that looks rather like an elephant's trunk.

**Leaves:** Basal leaves narrowly elliptical, 5-25 cm long, deeply cleft into rows of serrate lobes, creating a fern-like appearance.

**Habitat:** Wet mountain meadows from mid- to high elevations.

**Range:** B.C. to California.

# SMALL-FLOWERED PAINTBRUSH

*Castilleja parviflora*

**Plant:** An upright, unbranched perennial 15-30 cm tall, often with several adjacent flower stems.

**Flower:** Color can be white or red, what appears to be the petals in all paintbrushes are actually bracts around the flower, these bracts are 12-25 mm long in this species.

**Leaves:** 1-4 cm long, cleft into several deep lobes, the central lobe the widest.

**Habitat:** Subalpine meadows and high elevation stream banks.

**Range:** Alaska to Oregon.

73

## SPREADING PHLOX

*Phlox diffusa*

**Plant:** A mat-forming perennial typically 4-8 cm tall.

**Flower:** 5 spreading pink, lavender or white petals, each 5-9 mm wide, each flower 1-2 cm wide.

**Leaves:** Linear, pointed at the tip, 5-20 mm long, opposite one another on the stem.

**Habitat:** Rocky slopes, ridges and outcrops from mid- to alpine zones.

**Range:** B.C. to California.

## SICKLETOP LOUSEWORT, LEAFY LOUSEWORT

*Pedicularis racemosa*

**Plant:** An upright, multi-stemmed perennial 15-50 cm tall.

**Flower:** White to purple, 1-1.5 cm long, petals fused and twisted, with 3-25 flowers at the end of an erect flower stalk.

**Leaves:** Lanceolate, 4-10 cm long and 5-15 mm wide, doubly serrate, alternate along the stem.

**Habitat:** Moist open forests and meadows from mid- to subalpine elevations.

**Range:** B.C. to California.

# SNOW DOUGLASIA

*Douglasia nivalis*

**Plant:** A matted, cushion-forming perennial to 8 cm tall.

**Flower:** Five bright red to magenta-purple petals, fused together at the base, with 2-10 flowers together on short stems.

**Leaves:** 5-20 cm long, toothed, wider at the tip than at the base, covered with fine gray hairs.

**Habitat:** Sagebrush slopes to alpine ridges, usually in dry, rocky places at high elevatons.

**Range:** B.C. to Washington.

# SMOOTH DOUGLASIA

*Douglasia laevigata*

**Plant:** A low, spreading, matted perennial, the flower stalks 2-7 cm tall.

**Flower:** 5 pink to purple spreading petals fused together at the base, each petal 4-5 mm long, flowers in clusters of 2-8 at stem tips.

**Leaves:** 5-20 mm long, wider at the tip than at the base, hairless or with fine hairs only along the margins, in clusters at base of branches.

**Habitat:** Rocky alpine ridges to coastal slopes.

**Range:** Washington to Oregon.

## PINK MOUNTAIN HEATHER
*Phyllodoce empetriformis*

**Plant:** A matted shrub 10-40 cm tall.

**Flower:** Petals pink, fused into a bell-shaped corolla with very short, reflexed lobes, in nodding clusters at stem tips.

**Leaves:** Linear and evergreen, 8-16 mm long, crowded along the stems.

**Habitat:** Open high elevation forests and subalpine and alpine meadows.

**Range:** Alaska to California.

## ALASKAN BLUEBERRY
*Vaccinium alaskaense*

**Plant:** A branching shrub .5-1.5 m tall.

**Flower:** Pink, morbidly globose flowers 7 mm long, single in the leaf axils.

**Fruit:** A tasty blue-black berry 7-10 mm long.

**Leaves:** Elliptic, 2.5-6 cm long, the lower surface distinctly lighter than the upper.

**Habitat:** In moist forests west of the crest from low to subalpine zones, and along the coast.

**Range:** Alaska to Oregon.

# ALPINE BOG LAUREL

*Kalmia microphylla*

**Plant:** A low, spreading shrub 5-15 cm high.

**Flower:** 5 pink to rose colored petals, the flowers 10-12 mm across, in small clusters at stem tips.

**Leaves:** Lanceolate, 1-2 cm long, dark green above and gray-hairy below, leathery, opposite one another on stem.

**Habitat:** Wet meadows and bogs from lowlands to subalpine zone.

**Range:** Alaska to California.

# PUSSY PAWS

*Spraguea umbellata*

**Plant:** A perennial with leaves pressed to the ground and prostrate flower stems, 3-8 cm tall.

**Flower:** 2 sepals and 4 petals, all pink to white and 4-10 mm long, many flowers clustered in rounded, often prostrate heads at stem tip.

**Leaves:** In a basal rosette, oblanceolate and leathery, 1.5-5 cm long, frequently red-tinged.

**Habitat:** Ponderosa pine woodland to rocky alpine ridges, especially in dry, gravelly areas.

**Range:** B.C. to Baja California.

## KINNIKINNICK, BEARBERRY
*Arctostaphylos uva-ursi*

**Plant:** A prostrate, spreading shrub 5-15 cm tall.

**Flower:** Petals pink, fused together into an urn-shaped corolla 5 mm long, in few-flowered clusters at or near stem tips.

**Fruit:** Bright red berries 7-10 mm long.

**Leaves:** Obovate, 1.5-3 cm long, thick and leathery.

**Habitat:** Open, dry areas from lowlands to mountain ridges.

**Range:** Alaska to California.

## YOUTH-ON-AGE
*Tolmiea menziesii*

**Plant:** An erect perennial with flowering stems 30-80 cm tall.

**Flower:** The calyx (fused sepals) more evident than petals, about 1 cm long, green, rose or brown, flowers numerous along erect stem.

**Leaves:** Ovate, serrate, 3-10 cm long, shallowly 3-7 lobed, the few stem leaves smaller.

**Habitat:** Moist forests, stream banks, roadsides, low to midelevations.

**Range:** Alaska to California.

# CUSHION BUCKWHEAT
*Eriogonum ovalifolium*

**Plant:** A mat-forming perennial 5-25 cm tall.

**Flower:** Tiny corolla 3-4 mm long, cream to pink, dozens of small flowers gathered in round clusters 1-4 cm wide at end of upright stems.

**Leaves:** Basal, 5-20 mm long, elliptic to obovate, gray-hairy.

**Habitat:** Sage-steppe to alpine ridges, in dry, sandy and gravelly places.

**Range:** B.C. to California.

# WOODLAND BEARD-TONGUE
*Nothochelone nemorosa*

**Plant:** An erect perennial with several leafy, erect stems 40-80 cm tall.

**Flower:** Corolla (fused petals) pink-purple, 25-33 mm long and 1 cm wide at mouth, 1 to several on long stalks in leaf axils.

**Leaves:** Ovate, conspicuously serrate, 4-11 mm long, opposite one another on stem.

**Habitat:** In moist forests, and on moist, open rocky slopes from low to subalpine elevations.

**Range:** B.C. to California.

# WESTERN MEADOWRUE

*Thalictrum occidentale*

**Plant:** An erect perennial 40-100 cm tall, with male and female flowers on separate plants.

**Flower:** Flowers are wind-pollinated and therefore lack petals, female flowers with showy red pistils, male flowers with dangling purple anthers.

**Leaves:** Compound leaves divided into 3s in ulitmate segments, which are lobed and toothed and 1-3 cm long.

**Habitat:** Meadows, slide tracks, open forests from low to subalpine.

**Range:** B.C. to California.

# COLUMBIA LEWISIA

*Lewisia columbiana*

**Plant:** A tufted, succulent perennial 10-30 cm tall.

**Flower:** 7-9 white petals with pink lines, 5-13 mm long, 5-20 flowers at end of branching stem.

**Leaves:** Basal, oblanceolate, fleshy, numerous, 2-10 cm long.

**Habitat:** Exposed rock outcrops and ledges from mid- to high elevations.

**Range:** B.C. to California.

# EDIBLE THISTLE
*Cirsium edule*

**Plant:** An erect, spiny biennial or short-lived perennial 4.5-2 m tall.

**Flower:** Big, pink-purple composite heads 3-6 cm across, composed entirely of small disk flowers, bracts below head woolly-hairy.

**Leaves:** Lanceolate to oblong, 5-25 cm long, toothed, lobed and spiny.

**Habitat:** Moist open forests and meadows at mid- to subalpine elevations.

**Range:** B.C. to Oregon.

# BIRD'S-BEAK LOUSEWORT
*Pedicularis ornithorhyncha*

**Plant:** An tufted perennial with upright flower stalks 5-30 cm tall.

**Flower:** Corolla (fused petals) purple, 1-1.5 cm long, the upper petal lobe narrowed and twisted into the shape of a bird's beak, 5-30 flowers clustered at stem tip.

**Leaves:** In a basal rosette, narrowly elliptical, 3-12 cm long, several times deeply cleft into fern-like segments.

**Habitat:** Wet meadows and rocky slopes in subalpine to alpine zones.

**Range:** Alaska to Washington.

# SILKY PHACELIA

*Phacelia sericea*

**Plant:** A silky-hairy perennial with tufted leaves and erect flower stalks 10-30 cm tall.

**Flower:** Corolla (fused petals) dark blue or purple, 5-6 mm long with yellow anthers protruding, many flowers tightly clustered in a terminal head.

**Leaves:** Mostly basal, widely elliptical, 3-10 cm long, deeply cleft into narrow segments.

**Habitat:** Rocky areas in subalpine to alpine zones.

**Range:** B.C. to California.

LEGUMINOSAE · PEA FAMILY

# WESTERN HEDYSARUM

*Hedysarum occidentale*

**Plant:** An upright perennial with several branched stems 40-80 cm tall.

**Flower:** Reddish to purple, 16-22 mm long, with 20-80 flowers closely attached along an upright stalk.

**Leaves:** Pinnately compound, with 9-21 elliptical leaflets 1-3 cm long.

**Habitat:** Rocky slopes in alpine zone.

**Range:** Washington.

# BLUE CLEMATIS

*Clematis columbiana*

**Plant:** A perennial climbing or trailing vine, .5-5 m long.

**Flower:** Petals lacking but sepals showy, blue to red-purple, 3.5-6 cm long and pointed.

**Leaves:** Compound leaf divided into 3 leaflets, these ovate, 3-6 cm long, leaves and leaflets on stalks.

**Habitat:** Open woods and talus slopes from low to midelevations.

**Range:** B.C. to Oregon.

# CROWBERRY

*Empetrum nigrum*

**Plant:** A low, spreading evergreen shrub with woolly branches, 5-15 cm tall.

**Flower:** Tiny, about 3 mm long, purple brown, solitary on stems.

**Fruit:** Purple-black and round, 4-5 mm in diameter.

**Leaves:** Needle-like, 4-8 mm long, alternate on stem and in dense whorls.

**Habitat:** Low bogs and coastal heathlands, alpine rocky slopes.

**Range:** B.C. to Oregon.

## SHOWY JACOB'S LADDER

*Polemonium pulcherrimum*

**Plant:** Perennial with weak, erect or sprawling stems 5-30 cm tall.

**Flower:** Corolla (fused petals) blue, often with a yellow eye, 7-13 mm long, 5-20 flowers congested at stem tip.

**Leaves:** Pinnately compound with many (11-25) small leaflets, resembling rungs on a ladder.

**Habitat:** Moist shaded sites below timberline and open rocky places above.

**Range:** Alaska to California.

RANUNCULACEAE · BUTTERCUP FAMILY

## OREGON ANEMONE

*Anemone oregana*

**Plant:** A delicate, upright perennial 10-30 cm tall.

**Flower:** Petals lacking, but the 5-7 sepals petal-like, blue to purple, 1-2 cm long, with one flower per stem.

**Leaves:** Compound, with 3-7 elliptical, serrate leaflets, 3 leaves in whorl just below the flower.

**Habitat:** Moist forests and moist open slopes, at mid- to subalpine elevations.

**Range:** Washington to Oregon.

# DAVIDSON'S PENSTEMON
*Penstemon davidsonii*

**Plant:** A low, spreading, matted perennial with flowering stems 5-10 cm tall.

**Flower:** Corolla (fused petals) blue to purple-lavender, 2-3.5 cm long, with 2-10 flowers blooming together at stem tips.

**Leaves:** Small (5-15 mm long), firm and rounded, opposite one another on stem.

**Habitat:** Rocky ledges and slopes from mid- to alpine zones.

**Range:** B.C. to California.

# SMALL-FLOWERED PENSTEMON
*Penstemon procerus*

**Plant:** A tufted perennial with flowering stems 5-35 cm tall.

**Flower:** Corolla (fused petals) blue-purple, 6-11 mm long, flowers bloom in whorls around and at tip of stem.

**Leaves:** Variable in size, long-lanceolate to elliptical, 2-10 cm long, opposite one another on stem, margins entire (no serrations), upper leaves smaller.

**Habitat:** Dry meadows, open forests, rocky slopes, sage-steppe to alpine zones.

**Range:** Alaska to California.

85

## MOUNTAIN BOG GENTIAN

*Gentiana calycosa*

**Plant:** Erect perennial, typically with several unbranched, leafy stems 10-30 cm tall.

**Flower:** Corolla (fused petals) deep blue, 2-3.5 cm long, with five lobes, at stem tip.

**Leaves:** Ovate, 1-2.5 cm long, opposite one another on stem.

**Habitat:** Wet meadows and bogs at high elevations.

**Range:** B.C. to California.

## MONKSHOOD

*Aconitum columbianum*

**Plant:** An upright, branching perennial 1-2 m tall.

**Flower:** Dark blue and 2.5-3.5 cm high, the upper petal forming a distinct hood, with 5-30 flowers along the upper stem.

**Leaves:** Palmately compound, the largest up to 15 cm wide, deeply lobed and toothed with 3-5 segments.

**Habitat:** Moist woods and stream banks from mid- to subalpine elevations.

**Range:** Alaska to California.

# COMMON HAREBELL

*Campanula rotundifolia*

**Plant:** An upright, branching perennial 10-70 cm tall.

**Flower:** Corolla distinctly bell-shaped, blue-purple, 1.5-3 cm long, with 5 lobes.

**Leaves:** Basal leaves rounded, the blade 1-2 cm, stem leaves linear, 1.5-8 cm long.

**Habitat:** Low to subalpine, in open forests, on grassy slopes and in rocky areas.

**Range:** Alaska to California.

# CASCADE PENSTEMON

*Penstemon serrulatus*

**Plant:** A perennial with upright stems 20-70 cm tall from a woody base.

**Flower:** Corolla deep blue, 17-25 mm, in tight clusters at stem tips.

**Leaves:** Ovate and sharply serrate, 3-8 cm long, opposite one another on stem.

**Habitat:** Moist, rocky slopes, open forests, meadows, from low to subalpine.

**Range:** B.C. to Oregon.

# COMMON BUTTERWORT

*Pinguicula vulgaris*

**Plant:** Tufted perennial basal leaves and naked flower stems 5-15 cm tall.

**Flower:** Corolla lavender-blue, 1.5-2.5 cm long, spurred, one flower per stem.

**Leaves:** All basal, succulent, oblanceolate, 2-5 cm long, slimy on the upper surface.

**Habitat:** Wet meadows, bogs, wet rocky ground from low to subalpine zones.

**Range:** Alaska to Oregon.

**Note:** This species is insectivorous, capturing insects on its sticky leaves.

# PURPLE SAXIFRAGE

*Saxifraga oppositifolia*

**Plant:** A ground-hugging perennial 2-4 cm high, 5-20 cm wide, seemingly plastered on rock surfaces.

**Flower:** 5 purple petals 7-9 mm long, flowers embedded in leafy mat.

**Leaves:** Obovate, 2.5-5 mm long, opposite one another in tight, matted clusters.

**Habitat:** Rock faces and crevices in the alpine zone.

**Range:** Alaska to Oregon.

# CUSICK'S SPEEDWELL

*Veronica cusickii*

**Plant:** An erect perennial 10-20 cm tall.

**Flower:** Corolla deep blue-violet with 4 spreading, asymmetrical lobes, 8-13 mm wide, with stamens and styles protruding more than 1 cm from center, flowers clustered at stem tips.

**Leaves:** Elliptic to ovate, 1-2.5 cm long, entire (not serrate), opposite one another on stem.

**Habitat:** Moist meadows, rocky slopes in subalpine and alpine zones.

**Range:** B.C. to Oregon.

# ALPINE SPEEDWELL

*Veronica wormskjoldii*

**Plant:** A perennial spreading from underground rhizomes, flower stems 5-25 cm tall.

**Flower:** Corolla pale blue with 4 spreading, asymmetrical lobes, 6-10 mm wide, with stamens and styles protruding less than 1 cm from center.

**Leaves:** Elliptic to ovate, 1-4 cm long, entire or lightly toothed, opposite on stem.

**Habitat:** Meadows, stream banks, moist slopes from subalpine to alpine elevations.

**Range:** Alaska to California.

# SHOWY ASTER

*Aster conspicuus*

**Plant:** An erect perennial 20-80 cm tall, spreading from underground rhizomes.

**Flower:** A composite head, the blue or violet rays 10-15 cm long, the eye yellow, with several to many blooms at stem tip.

**Leaves:** Firm and rough to the touch, ovate-elliptic and serrate, 6-18 cm long, sessile on stem (no stalk).

**Habitat:** In open coniferous forests, from low to moderate elevations.

**Range:** B.C. to Oregon.

# LOW MOUNTAIN LUPINE

*Lupinus lepidus*

**Plant:** A low, matted perennial 10-30 cm tall.

**Flower:** 8-13 mm long, often bi-colored, blue and white, in tight, erect clusters.

**Leaves:** Mostly basal, on long stalks, palmately compound, with 5-9 hairy leaflets.

**Habitat:** Dry, often rocky ground from lowlands to subalpine.

**Range:** B.C. to California.

# AMERICAN BROOKLIME

*Veronica americana*

**Plant:** An ascending perennial spreading from underground rhizomes, stems 10-80 cm long.

**Flower:** Corolla blue with 4 spreading, asymmetrical lobes, 5-10 mm wide, in elongate clusters emerging from leaf axils.

**Leaves:** Lance-shaped, 1.5-8 cm long, opposite one another on stem, all with short stalks.

**Habitat:** Wet ground and in shallow water, low to midelevations.

**Range:** Alaska to California.

# EARLY BLUE VIOLET

*Viola adunca*

**Plant:** A low, tufted, perennial 2-10 cm tall, spreading from underground rhizomes.

**Flower:** Violet to blue, 5-15 mm long, the lower 3 petals often white at the base, the spur often hooked.

**Leaves:** Lance-shaped, the blade 1-3 cm long, on long stalks.

**Habitat:** Dry to moist meadows, forests, rocky ridges, lowlands to timberline.

**Range:** Alaska to California.

## SMALL FLOWERED FORGET-ME-NOT
*Myosotis laxa*

**Plant:** A weakly upright or lax annual to short lived perennial 10-40 cm tall.

**Flower:** Petals blue, the flowers 3-5 mm wide with a yellow eye, blooming progressively along upper stem.

**Leaves:** Lower ones oblanceolate and 1.5-8 cm long, smaller up the stem.

**Habitat:** Moist soil and shallow water, low to midelevations.

**Range:** B.C. to California.

## MOUNTAIN FORGET-ME-NOT
*Myosotis alpestris*

**Plant:** An upright, branching perennial 10-30 cm tall.

**Flower:** Petals blue, the flowers 8-12 mm across, with a yellow eye, in coiled clusters at top of hairy stems.

**Leaves:** Oblanceolate below, 4-10 cm, hairy, lanceolate and shorter above.

**Habitat:** Subalpine meadows, along streams in open forests.

**Range:** Alaska to Oregon.

## ALPINE FORGET-ME-NOT
*Eritrichium nanum*

**Plant:** A low cushion plant, 1-4 cm tall.

**Flower:** Petals blue, flowers 5-9 mm wide, with a yellow or rose-red ring in center.

**Leaves:** Basal, oblong to ovate, 5-10 mm long, hairy.

**Habitat:** Sandy and gravelly ridges and slopes at alpine elevations.

**Range:** Washington.

# GREEN FALSE HELLEBORE

*Veratrum viride*

**Plant:** A narrow, erect perennial 1-2 m tall.

**Flower:** Individual flowers are small (1-2 cm wide) and green, with many clustered on elongate, drooping stems.

**Leaves:** Large (10-35 cm) and elliptic, with parallel veins very evident.

**Habitat:** Wet meadows, bogs, open forests from lowlands to subalpine zone.

**Range:** Alaska to Oregon.

# BREWER'S MITREWORT

*Mitella breweri*

**Plant:** A perennial with 1 to several erect flower stalks 20-40 cm tall.

**Flower:** Flowers small (4 mm across) and greenish, the petals divided into thread-like segments, flowers 15-60 long erect stem.

**Leaves:** Rounded to heart-shaped, 4-8 cm wide and nearly as long, toothed.

**Habitat:** Moist open forests, wet meadows from mid- to subalpine elevations.

**Range:** B.C. to California.

93

# Index of Common and Scientific Names

**95**